THE TRANSFORMATION FORMULA

How to Create Your Own Luck and Win the Lottery of Life

MARIA FRANCU

ISBN: 979-8-9938922-0-7

Publisher: Ignite Motivation Press

Cover and interior design, illustrations: STUDIOCUDICIO

www.ignitemotivation.com

This book is intended for inspiration and personal transformation. It is not a substitute for professional, medical, psychological, financial, or legal advice.

Printed in the United States of America.

Table of Contents

CHAPTER 3

THE PRINCIPLES OF TRANSFORMATION

CHAPTER 4

CHAPTER 5:

For my daughters, Theodora and Tiffany.
My greatest teachers, my forever loves,
the living proof that transformation is real,
that beauty is born from courage,
and that love is the most sacred alchemy of all.

My Mission

To be a guide.
To help people rise, transform, and live their best lives.

I do not teach from a distance or speak from a pedestal.
I walk beside those I serve, as a companion in transformation.

I don't just transfer information;
I help awaken what is already alive within each person.

My work is to create a safe and sacred space,
where the inner fire can awaken to burn away
what no longer serves,
and to illuminate what is waiting to be born.

Transformation is not a lecture.
It is a lived journey.
And together, we walk it,
living by design and not by default.

PROLOGUE

The Birth of the Transformation Formula

The idea for this book was born at the Sydney Opera House, during a performance of Richard Strauss's *Metamorphosen.*

The Sydney Opera House was built without microphones. Every curve, surface, and material was engineered to reflect and carry sound naturally, allowing every listener to hear the same balanced tone. It is not a coincidence; it is physics and precision. The entire structure was designed for resonance.

As I sat there, surrounded by that sound, I realized something simple but profound: **human beings are built the same way.** Our minds, bodies, and emotions are systems of vibration. Every thought, word, and feeling sends out a frequency that interacts with everything around us. When these frequencies align, we feel clarity, coherence, and flow. When they don't, we experience distortion, what we call stress, fatigue, or conflict.

Metamorphosen is about transformation, how one phrase evolves into another, how motion creates meaning. Listening to it, I understood that transformation follows laws as precise as physics. Change is not random; it is structural. Just like the Opera House, our lives perform better when they are built for resonance.

Strauss composed this symphony when he was almost eighty years old, a living example of vitality, creativity, and human potential. We can continue to create, to evolve, and to live with purpose for as long as we are alive. Longevity, when aligned with clarity and intention, becomes a powerful design of both life and health span.

That evening, I felt that I was meant to be there. I hadn't planned to attend the concert; I didn't even have a ticket. I had come only for a one-hour tour, but when a last-minute seat became available, something inside me said *stay*. It was one of those unplanned moments that later felt designed, as if life itself had orchestrated the timing. For years I had been fascinated by, and studying, the subject of change, of evolution, of becoming and of how people grow, adapt, and rebuild themselves after life's turning points. And in that concert hall, all those ideas converged into one clear insight: awareness and emotion, not knowledge alone, ignite true transformation. **Knowledge reaches the mind, but vibration reaches the heart.**

That realization became the foundation of this book.

The Transformation Formula is not philosophy; it's design. It is a blueprint for building your inner architecture where thoughts, emotions, and actions move together in alignment, creating the music of your life with strength, clarity, and purpose.

Becoming Your Best Self by Design

HOW I GUIDE YOUR TRANSFORMATION

Above all, I am a guide. I walk beside you, not ahead of you and not behind you, as we design the path toward the life you were meant to live.

Transformation cannot be taught in theory. It must be learned and felt at the same time. Thought alone cannot transform, and feeling alone cannot sustain change. Transformation happens when thought and feeling fuse, when awareness meets emotion, when understanding becomes embodiment.

That's where I come in, to help you bring intention and design into every step of your becoming.

As a *Teacher*, I bring structure and clarity. I help you connect the dots, simplify the complex, and translate insight into practical action. I believe that knowledge becomes power only when it is lived. My role is to help you turn wisdom into rhythm, one small, conscious step at a time.

As a *Philosopher*, I invite depth and meaning. I help you look beneath the surface of your experiences to find the lesson, the truth, and the growth within them. Together, we explore the patterns that repeat in your life, not to analyze them endlessly, but to free you from them. Meaning transforms pain into purpose.

As a *Visionary*, I hold the higher design of your life. I help you see what is possible before it becomes visible. I remind you that you were never meant to live unconsciously; you were born to create intentionally. Together, we align your vision with your values and your actions with your purpose.

As a *Storyteller,* I bring emotional resonance. I speak to the heart as much as to the mind. Stories are the language of humanity; they awaken empathy, courage, and connection. Through stories, I help you remember that your life is not a series of random events but a living work of art.

As a *Provocateur*, I invite courage. I challenge limiting beliefs, disrupt complacency, and invite truth to the surface. Sometimes transformation requires being gently shaken awake, not to break, but to remember your strength. I will always hold the mirror steady until you are ready to see your full power.

This is how I serve. Through teaching, meaning, vision, story, and courage, I help you bridge thought and feeling, awareness and action, clarity and embodiment.

Transformation is not something I do to you; it's something we walk through together. You bring your life, your truth, and your desire to grow. I bring my energy, my experience, my knowledge, and my unwavering belief that you can rise.

Together, we create transformation, real, grounded, lasting.

Above all, I am here to guide you home to yourself and live a life by design and not by default.

THE JOURNEY AHEAD

This book is a companion for your journey, a mirror, a map, and a gentle guide.
It is not meant to be rushed. Each section invites reflection, honesty, and awareness.
You don't have to have everything figured out. You only need to begin.
The book unfolds in five chapters:

Chapter 1: Becoming Your Best Self by Design

This book is not about theory. It's about building a real system for change, one that turns ideas into actions and actions into results.

Most people want to improve their lives, but they rely on motivation alone. Motivation feels good, but it doesn't last.

What lasts is design, a clear formula that helps you understand yourself, focus your energy, and stay consistent.

Chapter 2: The Foundation of Transformation

Every transformation begins with something unseen yet essential, a foundation strong enough to hold growth. This section reveals what lies beneath change: the elements that give it form, purpose, and direction. Transformation is not built in a single moment but shaped through clarity, guided by values, directed by vision, and fueled by energy. Together, these four elements form the living foundation of your evolution, the ground from which your new design begins to rise.
Part 1 - Clarity: The Superpower of Transformation
Part 2 - Values & Needs: The Compass Within

Part 3 - Direction: Knowing Where You Are Going
Part 4 - Energy: The Force that Moves You

Chapter 3: The Principles of Transformation

Once you know where you are and why you want change, the principles show you how to bring your transformation to life day by day, choice by choice. It unfolds through two layers:

Part 1 - The Practice of Mastery: Integrity, Responsibility, Accountability, Courage, Vision, Focus, Faith, Contribution, Authenticity, Legacy

Part 2 - The Practice of Alignment: Less Is More, Slow Is Fast, Simple Is Complex, Team Is a Multiplier, Power Over Force

Chapter 4: The Tools of Transformation

The tools are where awareness becomes action and philosophy becomes practice.
They give structure, rhythm, and momentum to your design.

Part 1 - Turning Awareness into Action: Life Inventory, The North Star Map, The Energy Audit, The Willpower Compass, The Elimination and Delegation Matrix, The Accountability Partnership, The Reflection Journal, The Action Calendar, The Gratitude Ledger, The Morning Ritual, The Planning Practice, The Evening Reset

Part 2 - Turning Self Reflection into Clarity: The Mirror, The Inner Dialogue

Chapter 5: The Legacy

Every journey leaves a trace, a message, a meaning, a light to guide others. In this final section, you will explore *The Language of Symbols* and *The Three Forces of Life: Love, People, and Time.* You will close with reflection, gratitude, and the awareness that transformation never truly ends. It continues in the lives you touch, the energy you create, and the legacy you live each day.

Together, these layers bridge knowing and becoming. They turn your insight into rhythm, your awareness into structure, and your design into daily life.

Pause between sections. Write in the spaces. Let the questions work through you, not just for you.

Return to these pages whenever life feels ready for a reset, when you sense a shift, a calling, or a quiet desire to live with more intention.

This is not theory. It's practice. It's the art of becoming your best, one conscious step at a time, and living life by design and not by default.

Before We Begin

I wrote this book for you,
for the seekers of clarity, the builders of dreams, the alchemists of their own becoming.
For those who know there is more to life than surviving.
For the ones who feel something stirring within them, a quiet whisper asking for renewal.
For the rebuilders, the believers, and the brave souls who are ready to begin again.

For the ones whose hearts still believe in transformation,
who know that life is not a straight line but a sacred spiral of
becoming.
For all who sense that their life is meant to be designed, not
drifted,
a companion for the journey back to your essence,
and a gentle reminder that everything you seek has always lived
within you.

This book is your companion,
a guide back to your own light,
your foundation for transformation,
and your invitation to rise
and live by design and not by default.

BECOMING YOUR BEST SELF BY DESIGN

This book is **crafted** to help you transform awareness into action and energy into purpose, guiding you to become the best version of yourself.
It will teach you how to:

- See clearly where you are today (**Clarity**).

- Understand what matters most (**Values & Needs**).

- Define where you want to go (**Direction**).

- Activate the energy to get there (**Energy**).

- Live your truth through daily practice (**Principles**).

- Sustain transformation through structure and rhythm (**Tools**).

Each chapter offers reflection prompts, practical exercises, and small daily actions. The goal is not perfection but progress through presence.
By the time you finish, you will have:

- A personal **Life Inventory** and **North Star Map**.

- A clear set of **Principles** guiding your decisions.

- A customized set of **Tools** sustaining your growth.

- A renewed relationship with **energy, focus, and integrity**.

- The complete **Formula of Transformation,** a clear system of living by design and not by default.

- And, a life lived by design, not by default.

This book is not about changing who you are. It's about remembering who you were meant to be before the world told you otherwise.

FIRST STEP: HOW TO START

Before transformation begins, you must first create space for it.

This is not only about time or discipline. It's about energy.
When your outer world is cluttered, your inner world can't
breathe. Transformation begins not with thinking, but with
clearing.
You don't need to do everything at once. You simply need to
begin.

Step 1: Get a Notebook

This will be your sacred space, your *Transformation Journal*.
Write by hand when you can. There's something alchemical
about ink meeting paper, the moment thought becomes form.
If you prefer, use a digital space or even a dedicated ChatGPT
assistant to capture your reflections.
The important thing is to create a home for your awareness.

Step 2: Glance Through the Book

Glance through *The Transformation Formula* just to get a sense of
what it is about, then move to Step 3.
This is not a book just to read. It's a book to practice.

Step 3: Declutter Your Physical Life

Transformation begins in the visible world.
Start small and let each step prepare you for the next.

Begin with your car, a small, contained environment that mirrors
your mind.

Then move to your office space, where your mental and creative energy flows.
Next, your coat closet, living room, and kitchen, the daily layers of your life.
Finally, expand to your entire home or living space, every drawer, shelf, and corner where energy has become stagnant.

As you work, be fully present and intentional.
You are not just cleaning; you are clearing.
You are symbolically releasing the past to make space for what is meant to come.

Step 4: Listen to the Silence

As your space clears, your mind opens.
Ideas will begin to arrive, insights, dreams, direction.
Don't force them. Simply notice and write them down.
Each word you write is an act of creation, a signal to the universe that you are ready.

Step 5: Return to the Book and Begin the Practice

Now that your physical world is lighter, your inner world will have space to expand.
Return to the book and work with it intentionally. Reflect. Apply. Embody.
Transformation is not just read. It is lived.

Step 6: Remember, Transformation Is Not a Race

Go slowly. Be kind to yourself.
Transformation unfolds through reflection and awareness, consistency, and love.

Every small action brings you closer to the life you are meant to live.

Step 7: Read the Book Again and Practice It Again

When you finish your first journey through this book, begin again. This time, everything will feel different. You'll understand faster and more deeply.

You'll notice why certain words repeat so often: **reflection, awareness, clarity, alignment, action, rhythm, and "live by design, not by default."**

These repetitions are intentional. They carry energy and meaning. They are the rhythm of transformation itself.

Each rereading refines your understanding and strengthens your results.

Transformation isn't a single event; it's a living practice that grows with you.

YOUR QUICK-START CHECKLIST

- Get your *Transformation Journal.*
- Read *The Transformation Formula* once for understanding.
- Declutter your car.
- Declutter your office or workspace.
- Declutter your coat closet.
- Declutter your living room.
- Declutter your kitchen.
- Declutter your entire home and living space.
- Reflect and write your insights.
- Begin working with the book, one page, one day, one insight at a time.

You don't need to know how everything will happen. You just need to begin.

And, in that first act of beginning, your transformation has already begun.

Every time you return to this book, it will meet you at a higher level.
Your awareness will be sharper, your clarity deeper, and your rhythm stronger.
What once felt like effort will begin to feel like flow.
That is how transformation becomes mastery, one practice, one return, one conscious choice at a time.

CHAPTER 2

THE FOUNDATION OF TRANSFORMATION

PART 1

CLARITY: THE SUPERPOWER OF TRANSFORMATION

"A journey of a thousand miles begins with a single step." Lao Tzu

Every transformation begins with reflection and awareness.
Before you can design your life, you must see it clearly, not as you wish it to be, but as it truly is.
The Transformation Formula is a journey from seeing to becoming, from reflection and awareness to embodiment.
Each part builds on the last, Clarity, Values, Direction, and Energy, guiding you toward a life designed by choice, not by default.

Every transformation begins also with clarity.
You can't change what you can't see. Before you set goals or chase new dreams, first know exactly where you stand. Think of your life like a GPS: if it doesn't know your current location, it can't guide you anywhere.

That's where the power of inventory comes in. This first step isn't about judgment or comparison. It's about awareness.

Clarity is the *Phoenix*'s flame burning away illusion so truth can rise in its place. Clarity gives you the truth, and truth gives you direction. Without it, even the most inspired vision has no solid ground to stand on.

Today, you'll create your own **Life Inventory**, a simple, structured way to measure where you are, right now, across seven key areas of life. The clearer you see your present reality, the more powerful your transformation becomes.

Life Inventory: Where Am I Now?

1. Health & Energy

Morning Energy: □ Low □ Medium □ Elevated
Sleep Quantity (avg per night): □ 8 hrs □ 7 hrs □ 6 hrs □ <5 hrs

Sleep Quality: □ Poor □ Fair □ Good □ Excellent

Weight: _____ lbs / kg

Blood Pressure (last check): _____ / _____

Cholesterol (last check): _____ mg/dL

Vitamin D (last check): _____ ng/mL

Medical Checkup: □ Within last year □ More than 1 year ago

Exercise Frequency:

□ Rarely □ 1–2×/week □ 3–4×/week □ 5+×/week

Nutrition Quality:

□ Mostly processed □ Mix of both □ Mostly fresh, whole foods

Hydration (avg water intake):

□ <4 cups/day □ 4–7 cups/day □ 8+ cups/day

Daily Energy Curve: □ Frequent crashes □ Steady □ High sustained energy

2. Relationships & Belonging

Close Relationships (family/partner):

□ Strong & supportive □ Neutral □ Strained

Friendships (close friends I can call anytime):

□ 0 □ 1–2 □ 3–5 □ 6+

Social Support (I can count on others):

□ Always □ Sometimes □ Rarely

Belonging (to a group/community):

□ Yes, strongly □ Somewhat □ Not at all

Time Invested in Relationships:

□ Daily □ Weekly □ Monthly □ Rarely

Emotional Safety (I feel safe to be myself):

□ Yes □ Sometimes □ Rarely

Contribution to Others (hours/month): □ 0 □ 1–5 □ 6–10 □ 10+

3. Work & Purpose

Fulfillment at Work: □ Very fulfilling □ Somewhat □ Not at all

Alignment with Purpose: □ Strong □ Partial □ None

Work Stress Level: ☐ Low ☐ Moderate ☐ High

Work–Life Balance (hours worked/week):

☐ <30 ☐ 30–40 ☐ 40–50 ☐ 50+

Primary Income Satisfaction:

☐ More than enough ☐ Enough ☐ Not enough

Job Stability: ☐ Very secure ☐ Somewhat secure ☐ Unstable

Skill Use: ☐ I use my strengths daily ☐ Occasionally ☐ Rarely

Motivation: ☐ Excited most days ☐ Neutral ☐ Dread going to work

Career Growth: ☐ Advancing ☐ Plateaued ☐ Declining

4. Finances & Abundance

Financial Clarity: ☐ Clear picture of income/expenses

☐ Somewhat clear ☐ No clarity

Debt Situation: ☐ None ☐ Manageable ☐ Overwhelming

Savings/Investments: ☐ Consistent ☐ Some ☐ None

401(k) Balance: $ _____

FICO Score (last check): _____

Net Worth (assets – liabilities): $ _____

Emergency Fund (months of expenses): ☐ 0 ☐ 1–3 ☐ 3–6 ☐ 6+

Financial Stress: ☐ Rarely worried ☐ Sometimes ☐ Often

Living Within Means: ☐ Yes ☐ Sometimes ☐ No

5. Growth & Learning

Learning New Skills: ☐ Actively enrolled in course/program
☐ Self-taught ☐ Not learning

Books/Podcasts (per month): ☐ 0 ☐ 1–2 ☐ 3–5 ☐ 6+

Personal Development Investment (time/week):
☐ 0 hrs ☐ 1–2 hrs ☐ 3–5 hrs ☐ 6+ hrs

Challenging Myself (outside comfort zone):
☐ Regularly ☐ Sometimes ☐ Rarely

Sense of Progress:
☐ Strong momentum ☐ Slow growth ☐ Stagnant

6. Lifestyle & Joy

Daily Joy/Play: ☐ Every day ☐ Weekly ☐ Rarely

Hobbies (hours/week): ☐ 0 ☐ 1–3 ☐ 4–6 ☐ 7+

Vacations/Trips (past year): ☐ 0 ☐ 1–2 ☐ 3–4 ☐ 5+

Home Environment:
☐ Inspiring & supportive ☐ Neutral ☐ Stressful/draining

Financial Freedom for Lifestyle:

☐ Can afford most desires ☐ Some ☐ Very limited

Alignment with Values: ☐ Strong ☐ Partial ☐ Not aligned

7. Spirituality & Inner Self

Connection with Inner Self: ☐ Strong ☐ Occasional ☐ Weak

Spiritual Practices (prayer, meditation, reflection): ☐ Daily

☐ Weekly ☐ Rarely ☐ Never

Gratitude Practice: ☐ Daily ☐ Sometimes ☐ Rarely

Journaling/Reflection (per week): ☐ 0 ☐ 1–2 ☐ 3–5 ☐ Daily

Sense of Peace: ☐ Often peaceful ☐ Sometimes ☐ Rarely

Meaning & Purpose Beyond Self: ☐ Clear ☐ Somewhat ☐ Absent

Keeping It Simple

Think of it this way, computers run on just two numbers: 0 and 1. Just two simple digits, and yet from them, entire worlds are created. Your phone, the internet, even this book, all born from simplicity itself.

Transformation compounds quietly, like small actions multiplying over time. It is essential to keep it simple. Complete your inventory with honesty. Clarity doesn't require perfection, only awareness. Over time, the results will be greater than you can imagine.

Closing Reflection

This is your clarity map, not a judgment or a grade, simply the truth of where you are today. The power of this exercise lies in awareness. As you can see, awareness is paramount. Once you see your present clearly, you can design your future by choice.

Awareness is the raw material.
Action is the _alchemy_.
Together they create transformation.

"Clarity precedes mastery." Robin Sharma

In the next part titled "Values & Needs: The Compass Within" we'll go deeper.
You'll uncover the values that guide you, the needs that fuel you, and the thoughts that shape your direction.

Live by Design, Not by Default.

PART 2

VALUES & NEEDS: THE COMPASS WITHIN

"Knowing yourself is the beginning of all wisdom." Aristotle

In *"Clarity: The Superpower of Transformation,"* I invited you to look honestly at where you are, the outer landscape of your life. You created your first Life Inventory and brought clarity to your reality.

Now, it's time to turn inward.

If clarity is the light of rebirth, the flame that awakens the *Phoenix* within, your values and needs are the *Compass* and magnetic field that show you which direction to go. Because even when you have a map, you can still feel lost if you don't know which way is true north.

Your Inner Compass

Imagine holding a compass in your hand. No matter where you stand, in the desert, the forest, or the middle of a storm, the needle always finds its way back to north.

Your values quietly orient you toward what truly matters. Your needs are the magnetic field that moves the needle, the unseen forces that drive your behaviors and emotions. And your thoughts are the wind around the compass, shaping how your values and needs express themselves.

When your values, needs, and thoughts are aligned, you move with clarity and confidence. When they pull in different directions, you feel stuck, no matter how hard you try. True transformation unfolds gently, like the _Butterfly_, through awareness, patience, and inner alignment.

True transformation begins when your values, needs and thoughts speak the same language. That's when alignment is born.

Why Most People Feel Lost

Many people have never defined their values or understood their core needs.
They chase success, approval or comfort, not realizing that what they're really seeking is the fulfillment of an unspoken need.

We're taught how to succeed, but not how to align. We measure progress by what we have, not by how we feel.

Before you set a direction or define goals, uncover your _Compass_: your values (what matters), your needs (what sustains you), and your thoughts (the energy that guides you).

Part 1: The Values Inventory, What Truly Matters to You

Your values are the invisible threads that weave your life together. They shape decisions, relationships, and meaning.

When you live in alignment with your values, life feels steady. When you don't, you feel tension and confusion even if everything "looks good."

Step 1: Identify Your Core Values
Read the list below and highlight the ones that resonate deeply:

Achievement • Adventure • Authenticity • Balance • Beauty • Compassion • Connection • Contribution • Courage • Creativity • Discipline • Family • Freedom • Friendship • Fun • Growth • Health • Honesty • Integrity • Joy • Kindness • Learning • Love • Order • Peace • Recognition • Security • Service • Spirituality • Success • Trust • Wisdom

Step 2: Narrow It Down

Choose 10 that feel most important.

From those, select 5.

Then choose your Top 3 Core Values, the non-negotiables.

Reflection Questions:

– Which values have guided me at my best?

– Which, when ignored, have caused pain or regret?

Step 3: Reflect on Alignment

Ask yourself:

- Am I living these values daily?
- Where are they reflected in my life?
- Where are they missing?

Awareness of these gaps is not failure, it's power. Once you see where your values are honored or ignored, you can realign your energy.

Part 2: The Needs Inventory, What Fuels You

If values are your compass, needs are the fuel that keep you moving.
When your needs are met in healthy ways, you feel energized.
When they're unmet or met in unhealthy ways, you feel drained.

Step 1: Rate Your Needs (1 - 10)

Rate each of the six core human needs from 1 (low) to 10 (high) based on how fulfilled it feels in your life today.

1. Stability / Grounding
The need to feel anchored in safety, trust, and consistency, to know that your life has a reliable foundation. Stability creates inner calm and emotional balance from which growth can flourish.

2. Variety / Expansion

The need for freshness, novelty, and adventure, to experience the unknown and awaken creativity. Expansion keeps life vibrant and prevents the soul from shrinking into comfort.

3. Significance / Purpose

The need to feel seen, valued, and meaningful, to know that your presence matters. True significance isn't born of comparison but of contribution, being a light in the lives of others.

4. Connection / Love

The need to belong, to give and receive love, and to feel understood. Connection is the bridge between souls; it reminds us that we are not meant to walk alone.

5. Growth / Evolution

The need to learn, stretch, and become more of who you are. Growth is the heartbeat of transformation. It keeps you moving toward your highest potential.

6. Contribution / Impact

The need to give beyond yourself, to leave the world better than you found it. Contribution turns energy into legacy, it's how love continues after you.

Note: The framework of six core human needs draws inspiration from widely recognized models in psychology and coaching. The interpretations and applications presented here are my own original synthesis within The Transformation Formula.

Step 2: Identify Dominant and Unmet Needs

Mark your top 2 highest and bottom 2 lowest scores.

Reflect:
– How am I meeting each need?
– Are my methods healthy or draining?
– What new habits could meet these needs better?

Step 3: Notice the Patterns
Behaviors are often strategies to meet needs:

Overworking → Significance
People pleasing → Connection
Controlling → Stability
Change the strategy, not just the behavior.

Integration: Alignment of Values, Needs & Thoughts

You've now mapped three inner layers:

· Values - what matters most.

· Needs - what fuels you.

· Thoughts - the stories that steer you.

When all three align, decisions flow naturally. You stop pushing against yourself and begin moving in harmony with your truth.

Closing Reflection

Awareness is the beginning of all alignment. When you know your values, you know what matters. When you understand your needs, you know what sustains you. When you observe your thoughts, you can choose a better story. This is where awareness becomes transformation, the sacred work of the inner _Alchemist_.

Together, they create the inner architecture of your life, the bridge between intention and action.

Take a moment to reflect:

- Which of my top values am I honoring or neglecting?
- Which needs are being met or unmet?
- What is my inner dialogue telling me each day?

This is the clarity that leads to direction.
"Until you make the unconscious conscious, it will direct your life and you will call it fate." Carl Jung

In the next part titled "Knowing Where You Are Going", we'll connect the dots.
You'll use your clarity, values, and needs to chart your future, your own *North Star* and the life you design by choice, not by default.

Live by Design, Not by Default.

PART 3

DIRECTION: KNOWING WHERE YOU ARE GOING

> *"The best way to predict your future
> is to create it."* Peter Drucker

In *"Clarity: The Superpower of Transformation,"* you looked honestly at where you are, the outer landscape of your life.
In *"Values & Needs: The Compass Within,"* you uncovered what matters most, the internal *Compass* that guides your energy and decisions.

Now, it's time to lift your eyes to the horizon, to the place where intention becomes direction and clarity becomes motion. Like the *Phoenix*, you rise from what was, ready to create what will be.

Once you know where you are and what matters to you, the next question is inevitable: Where do you want to go?

The North Star

For centuries, sailors have relied on one constant light to find their way across vast oceans, the *North Star*. Even when storms blurred the horizon or clouds hid the moon, they knew that, for as long as they could find that light, they would not be lost.

In life, your north star is your vision, the clear image of the life you want to create, the person you are becoming, and the direction that gives meaning to your steps.

It doesn't need to be loud or perfect; it just needs to be yours. Your north star doesn't bend to trends or pressure. It stays steady as you evolve, quietly guiding you back when life gets noisy or uncertain.

The "Why" is Your Fuel for Direction

Every journey begins with a spark: that quiet why inside your heart. It's the reason you want what you want, the meaning behind your goals, and the energy that turns intention into persistence.

Without your why, even the best plan fades. When your why is steady, you can walk through uncertainty with courage, because purpose becomes the engine behind every step.

Think of your why as your fuel. Your direction is where you're going, but your why is what keeps you moving when progress feels slow or challenges appear.

Connecting With Your "Why"

To find your why, begin by looking at your goals.

For every desire, ask yourself:

- Why do I want this?

- What feeling am I truly seeking?

- If I already had this, how would my life feel different?

Most people want success, freedom, or love but what they're truly seeking is a feeling: peace, safety, contribution, belonging, or joy.

When your goals are powered by feelings that align with your values and needs, you stop chasing achievements that drain you and start building a life that sustains you.

The Emotional Engine of Purpose

Purpose is emotional, not intellectual.
It lives in the heart, not in the checklist.

Ask yourself:

- Which of my values do I want to live more fully?

- Which of my needs feel most alive when I'm at my best?

- Where in my life do I already feel in flow, and what's fueling that?

This is your internal calibration, the merging of clarity and alignment into direction.

When your direction is powered by purpose, it no longer depends on motivation. Motivation fades. Meaning endures.

Transformation, like the _Butterfly_, unfolds quietly through trust, patience, and devotion to your purpose.

"He who has a why to live can bear almost any how." Friedrich Nietzsche

The "How": Turning Vision into Motion

Once you know where you want to go and why it matters, the next step becomes simple: you begin to move one small, intentional step at a time.

Big dreams are never built in one leap. They are shaped in the quiet repetition of small choices, compounded over time.

The Compounding Effect

Imagine two options:

Option 1: Receive $1 million today.

Option 2: Start with one penny that doubles every day for 30 days.

At first, the penny seems insignificant.
By day 10, it's only a few dollars.
By day 20, just over $5,000.
But by day 30, it becomes more than $5 million.

That's the power of consistency compounded over time.
It's the same with your habits, your focus, your energy.

What seems invisible today becomes unstoppable tomorrow.

Your job is not to do everything. It's to do the right small things, every day, in alignment with your direction.

Designing Your Horizon

To bring your direction to life, I invite you to work with four levels of time, the bridge between vision and action:

1. Daily: What one action today supports my direction?
Example: drink more water, write for 15 minutes, connect with someone, move your body.

2. Weekly: What themes or habits do I want to strengthen?
Example: consistency in movement, time for creativity, dollar-cost average investing.

3. Medium-Term (6–12 months): What goals will reflect my progress?
Example: completing a course, saving a specific amount, improving health, strengthening relationships.

4. Long-Term (3–5 years): What is the larger picture I am building toward?
Example: a new career, a meaningful project, financial independence, or a lifestyle by design.

When each horizon aligns with your values and your why, life begins to move naturally, with ease, not force.

Your Direction Map

Take a journal and reflect on these prompts:

- My North Star Vision: What is the big picture I'm moving toward?

- My 3 Core Goals: What goals best align with my values and needs right now?

- My Next Step: What small action will I take this week to move in that direction?

That's all it takes, clarity, purpose, and the next aligned step. Then another. And another.

This is how transformation becomes real. It is the moment vision turns into creation, guided by the inner _Alchemist_, who turns intention into form, one deliberate step at a time.

Walking Toward Your North Star

Every transformation begins with a single moment of awareness and continues with one conscious step at a time. You live intentionally when you know where you are, you understand who you are, and you choose where you're going next.

In **"Clarity**: _The Superpower of Transformation,"_ you looked clearly at your present reality.
In **"Values & Needs**: _The Compass Within,"_ you uncovered the inner guidance that aligns your thoughts, values, and needs.
Now, **in** **"Direction**: _Knowing Where You Are Going"_, you've lifted your eyes toward the horizon to design your next chapter with intention.

Your north star will continue to evolve as you do, and as long as your steps are anchored in clarity, alignment, and purpose, you will always be moving in the right direction, even when the path bends or slows.

Closing Reflection

Remember, direction is not about speed, it's about truth.
Your truth. Your rhythm. Your design.

Begin today.
Take one step, however small, toward your north star.
The path will rise to meet you.

"The future depends on what you do today." Mahatma Gandhi

Live by Design, Not by Default.

PART 4

Energy: The Force That Moves You

"Energy and persistence conquer all things." Benjamin Franklin

You now know where you are and where you're going.

The final step is to bring it all to life, to awaken the force that moves your dreams from vision to form. Because clarity without energy remains an idea, and direction without motion stays a map. **Energy** is the current that makes your design move.

In *"Clarity: The Superpower of Transformation"*, you looked honestly at where you are, the outer landscape of your life.
In *"Values & Needs: The Compass Within"*, you uncovered what matters most, the internal Compass that guides your energy and decisions.
In *"Direction: Knowing Where You Are Going"*, you lifted your eyes to your North Star, your vision for the future.

Now, it's time to activate the invisible current that will carry you there, because no dream moves forward without energy. Energy is the unseen fire of the *Phoenix*, the force that turns clarity into motion and purpose into power.

The Invisible Current

Everything you do either gives you energy or takes it away. Every thought, every word, every interaction is an exchange. Energy is not just emotion or mood; it's the currency of transformation.

Before you can change your life, you must learn to manage your voltage. Reflection and awareness are the first steps. After each activity, ask yourself: Did this lift me or lower me? That simple question reveals your energetic truth.

Push vs. Pull

There are two ways to move through life.

Push energy is effort without alignment. It relies on willpower, discipline, and force. It swims against the current, and over time it exhausts you. You "should" push yourself forward and forward feels heavy.

Pull energy is alignment in motion. It feels magnetic, fluid, and synchronistic, like the movement of the _Butterfly_, graceful and effortless when you trust your wings. When your clarity, values, and direction are aligned, life begins to move with ease. You're no longer forcing progress; you're being drawn toward it.

Push drains. Pull sustains. Design your life for pull.

Managing Your Voltage

Friction means anything that makes a good habit harder to start. When you remove those tiny barriers, your behavior flows more easily, and you enter pull energy instead of push energy. This is how you design for flow.

1. Ways to reduce friction for what fuels you:

    · Lay out your workout clothes or tennis shoes the night before, it's easier to move in the morning.

    · Keep a water bottle on your desk, you hydrate more without willpower.

    · Place your journal or gratitude notebook on your nightstand, reflection happens naturally.

    · Keep healthy snacks visible, you make better choices without effort.

2. Ways to increase friction for what drains you:

Make energy depleting habits less convenient so that your awareness can step in.

    · Log out of social media apps or move them off your home screen and you interrupt mindless scrolling.

    · Keep your phone out of reach during meals or creative work and you protect focus and connection.

    · Delay email notifications or use "Do Not Disturb" hours and you reclaim mental peace.

    · Remove junk food from your house and you remove temptation instead of fighting it.

This creates just enough pause to break automatic patterns that drain energy. You're shaping your environment to serve your energy, not your impulses. When you lower resistance for what gives you life and raise resistance for what depletes it, you live by design, not by default, quite literally.

Reducing friction for what fuels your energy makes it easy to begin. Increasing friction for what drains your energy makes it easy to pause.

The Power of Leverage through Systems

Leverage is the quiet multiplier of energy. It's how you achieve more with less effort, how one action begins to create many results. Systems are the structures that make leverage possible.

Think of a system as a current that carries you forward: a ritual, a habit, a checklist, a calendar block, a workflow. Once in place, it keeps moving even when your motivation pauses.

Systems create synergy. They compound the energy you invest, turning consistency into momentum and momentum into flow.

The more intentional your systems, the more they do the work for you. Your routines become rhythm and cadence. Your structure becomes freedom.

Just as a lever allows you to lift something heavier with less force, a system allows you to sustain something greater with less strain. When clarity, alignment, and direction meet structure, effort transforms into ease. You're no longer pushing; you're being carried, pulled forward by design.

This is the power of leverage through systems, the art of designing your life to run on energy, not exhaustion.

The Law of Resonance: Energy Meets Energy

The Law of Resonance says that energy attracts energy of a similar frequency. What you think, feel, and embody sends a signal and the universe responds in kind.

When your internal state resonates with clarity, gratitude, and purpose, you begin to meet people, opportunities, and ideas that match that vibration. Life starts speaking your language.

This is why synchronicities appear when you're aligned. They're not coincidences; they're confirmations. The clearer your frequency, the cleaner your field, the faster resonance works.

You don't chase; you attract. You don't force; you align. Awareness of resonance transforms effort into magnetism. It's the invisible collaboration between you and the universe, and each moment of alignment is like winning life's lottery.

Why Some People Seem Lucky

Some people appear lucky, but what we call luck is often resonance in action. They are simply tuned in to a frequency of possibility and openness. Their energy is clear, their intention steady, their systems aligned, and opportunities recognize them.

"Lucky" people notice connections that others overlook. They follow intuition, trust timing, and act when the window opens.

Luck isn't random. It's readiness meeting resonance. The more aligned your inner world becomes, the more often life seems to "favor" you because you've learned to dance with its rhythm.

Manifestation: The Visible Form of Resonance

Manifestation isn't magic; it's resonance made visible. When your thoughts, emotions, and actions vibrate in harmony, the physical world reorganizes that and works to match your frequency. You become the _Alchemist_, turning invisible energy into visible creation through presence, clarity, and purpose.

It begins with clarity. It gains strength through emotion, the feeling of already having it. It becomes real through action, small, consistent, intentional steps that anchor energy into matter.

You manifest through coherence, not control. Through openness, not obsession.

The moment you align your energy with your vision, life begins to move in your favor. You recognize signs, meet allies, and find yourself in the right place at the right time.

Manifestation is simply energy remembering its potential, once you, the conscious co-creator, give it direction.

The Energy Audit

For one day, keep a small note on your phone or a card in your pocket. After each activity, mark it with a symbol:

(+) for energizing, (=) for neutral, and (–) for draining.

By evening, you'll see your energetic map, the hidden architecture of your day. Shift one minus to a plus, and you begin rewriting your voltage.

Closing Reflection

You began this journey by looking inward, by learning to see yourself with honesty and awareness.

Now, as you reach the end of *The Foundation of Transformation*, perspective shifts.
What once felt like your story now becomes the story of all things, the rhythm of life itself, written in nature.
The same intelligence that moves through your choices is the one that spins the galaxies.

We are stardust.

The universe is 13.8 billion years old, and the atoms in your body were once born inside stars that exploded and scattered their light across space.
You are literally made of stardust and remembering this changes everything.

You are not separate from energy. You are energy, taking human form.
The same laws that move galaxies also move through your heartbeat, your breath, your creative flow.

When you live in harmony with these laws, life moves with you, not against you.

You stop pushing and you begin to rise, carried by the same current that shaped the stars.
Energy is the bridge between knowing and becoming, the current that carries transformation.
Protect it. Direct it. Design for pull.

When your life and your energy match, the world aligns in rhythm with your heartbeat, and everything that once felt out of reach begins to find its way to you.

"The secret of change is to focus all your energy, not on fighting the old, but on building the new." Socrates

Live by Design, Not by Default.

CHAPTER 3

THE PRINCIPLES OF TRANSFORMATION

PART 1

The Practice of Mastery

"The unexamined life is not worth living." Socrates

You've now reached the summit of the first journey.
Clarity helped you see.
Values and Needs helped you align.
Direction gave you vision.
Energy brought it all to life.

But motion without guidance can scatter, and power without principle can fade.

The next stage of transformation asks for something deeper, structure, ethics, and truth in motion. Because energy alone creates speed, but principles create purpose.
This is where the journey turns from movement to meaning, from force to flow, from energy to mastery.

And mastery begins here.

Energy creates motion and principles create direction.
Without principles, energy scatters; with them, it becomes strength.
The Principles of Transformation are the architecture of a life by design, the invisible code that turns awareness into integrity and energy into mastery.

This is where power becomes character, and character becomes alignment.

1. Integrity

Integrity is being true to yourself in thoughts, words, and actions. It's when what you say, what you believe, and what you do are one and the same. It's not something you *have*; it's something you *live in*. Integrity means alignment.

When You Are In Integrity, You:

- follow your plan to save money, track expenses, skip impulse buys, and pay yourself first.
- say health matters, and your pantry, plate, and sleep schedule show it.
- tell the truth even when it's uncomfortable because honesty is important.
- say relationships matter, and you listen, keep promises, and show up when you're needed.
- keep the commitment to move your body even on hard days because discipline matters.

When You Are Not In Integrity, You:

- talk about saving but spend emotionally or "just this one."

- promise yourself a healthy week and end it with excuses.

- avoid difficult conversations and pretend things are fine.

- preach kindness but gossip about others.

- say you'll wake up early or work out but hit snooze again.

Practical Actions

1. Run an Integrity Audit.
   Pick three areas: money, health, and relationships.
   Under each, write two columns: "What I say I want" and "What I actually do."
   Notice where your behavior doesn't match your intention, that's where integrity is missing.

2. Create Alignment Plans.
   Choose one mismatch from each column and make a micro-plan to correct it:

   - Finance: "I'll transfer $50 automatically to savings every Friday."

   - Health: "I'll walk 20 minutes after lunch every day."

   - Relationships: "I'll call my friend instead of texting once a week."

3. Check Daily Alignment.
   Each evening, ask: "Did my actions today match my intentions?"
   If not, don't judge, adjust. Integrity is recalibration, not punishment.

Integrity is the first bridge from awareness to action. In *The Transformation Formula* you clarified your values and needs. Integrity is how you live them. It's the daily test of design over default. When your words and actions finally match, energy flows freely, and self-trust returns.

2. Responsibility

Responsibility is ownership. What happens in your life is up to you, not to luck, people, or circumstances. When you take responsibility, you reclaim power.

When You Are In Responsibility, You:

- are late once and you adjust your morning routine instead of blaming traffic.

- make a mistake at work, own it, and fix it instead of hiding it.

- notice your energy drops and decide to rest or move, you don't wait for someone to rescue you.

When You Are Not In Responsibility, You:

- explain your results by saying "I didn't have time."
- talk about what they should have done differently.
- repeat the same pattern and call it bad luck.

Practical Actions

1. Name one area where you feel stuck. Write one sentence that starts with "I am responsible for..."

   - Example: "I am responsible for creating more structure in my mornings."

2. Replace complaints with corrections. Every time you catch yourself blaming, pause and ask, "What can I do differently next time?"

3. Close your day with a check-in. Before bed, write three things you did right today and one you'll improve tomorrow. That's responsibility in motion.

Responsibility is where clarity becomes choice. In *The Foundation of Transformation*, you learned to see your patterns and energy leaks. Responsibility is applying that awareness, turning "I know" into "I do." It's the daily decision to design, not default.

3. Accountability

Accountability means being answerable first to yourself, then to others. It's the practice of keeping your word visible. When you hold yourself accountable, you turn goals into actions and promises into progress.

When You Are In Accountability, You:

- set a fitness goal and track every workout, even the short ones.
- tell your team or partner your deadlines and meet them.
- share your financial goals with someone who will check in.
- follow through on commitments, even when no one reminds you.
- review your week honestly and celebrate effort, not excuses.

When You Are Not In Accountability, You:

- keep your goals secret and no one notices when you stop.

- rationalize missed deadlines and call them "bad timing."

- tell yourself you'll start again Monday, every Monday.

- avoid feedback because it makes you uncomfortable.

- forget what you promised yourself two days after saying it.

Practical Actions

1. Create a Mirror System.
   Tell one person your top goal for the week. Ask them to check in every Friday, and make an assessment: yes or no, done or not done. Accountability grows stronger when shared.

2. Use Visible Tracking.
   Post your progress where you can see it, a wall calendar, notes app, or whiteboard. Seeing your streak builds pride and discipline.

3. Review Every Sunday.
   Write:

   - One promise I kept.

   - One promise I broke.

   - One change I'll make this week.

This short reflection closes each week with honesty, the seed of trust.

In *The Foundation of Transformation*, awareness created clarity. Accountability creates consistency. Clarity without accountability fades; accountability turns clarity into structure. It's the practice of walking your talk, one measured step at a time.

4. Courage

Courage isn't about being fearless. It's about acting even when fear is loud.
It's the decision to move forward while your hands still shake.
Courage is the bridge between intention and action.

When You Are In Courage, You:

- apply for the job, send the message, or ask the question even when your voice trembles.

- say no to what doesn't serve you, even if it disappoints others.

- try again after failing, because you value growth over comfort.

- tell the truth instead of saying what's easy.

- ask for help instead of pretending you have it all together.

When You Are Not In Courage, You:

- stay in a relationship, job, or habit that drains you because it feels "safe."

- postpone the dream until "later", a later that never comes.

- let fear of judgment silence your real opinion.

- scroll, binge, or distract yourself instead of taking the next hard step.

- know the truth but avoid acting on it.

Practical Actions

1. Do the Hard Thing First.
   Each morning, identify one task that scares or stretches you and do it before noon. Momentum kills fear faster than motivation ever can.

2. Name the Fear.
   Write it down: "I'm afraid that if I try, I'll fail / be judged / lose control."
   Naming the fear removes its fog; clarity restores power.

3. Create a Courage Log.
   At day's end, write one sentence: "Today I showed courage when...".
   Seeing proof builds trust in your strength and fear begins to shrink.

In *The Foundation of Transformation*, you learned how energy follows intention. Courage is where intention ignites movement.

It turns clarity into change and design into progress. Without courage, every plan remains theory. With courage you cross into action and expansion.

5. Vision

Vision gives direction to your energy. It's the picture of the life you want, clear enough to move you, real enough to guide you. Without vision, even hard work has no compass.

When You Are In Vision, You:

- know what you're working toward and can describe it in one sentence.
- plan your week around what matters most instead of reacting to what's loudest.
- make decisions based on long-term gain, not short-term comfort.
- visualize the outcome before taking the first step.
- remind yourself daily why this goal matters.

When You Are Not In Vision, You:

- say you want "more" but can't define what more means.

- start projects but lose interest because the end point is blurry.

- copy other people's goals instead of creating your own.

- fill your calendar but not your purpose.

- feel busy yet directionless like running without a map.

Practical Actions

1. Write Your One-Year Vision.
   In one paragraph, describe where you want to be 12 months from now.
   Be specific: Where are you? How do you feel? Who are you with? What have you built? Read it every morning.

2. Define the Why.
   After writing your vision, ask: Why does this matter to me? The stronger the reason, the longer the endurance.

3. Reverse-Engineer the Path.
   Break the vision into milestones:

   - 3 months → first checkpoint

   - 6 months → progress review

   - 12 months → result

In *The Foundation of Transformation*, clarity helped you understand who you are; vision helps you decide where you're going. It channels your energy into a single direction and turns dreams into measurable steps. Vision transforms possibility into a plan.

6. Focus

Focus is the discipline of attention. It's how you direct your energy toward what truly matters and protect it from what doesn't. Without focus, even effort gets diluted; with it, small actions create big results.

When You Are In Focus, You:

- start your day knowing your top three priorities and finish them first.
- keep your phone out of reach during deep work.
- say no to tasks that don't serve your goals.
- block time for what fuels you not just what demands you.
- leave space in your schedule for thinking, not just doing.

When You Are Not In Focus, You:

- multitask and call it productivity.
- check notifications before finishing a sentence.
- fill your calendar with other people's urgencies.
- confuse motion with progress.
- end the day busy but unsure what you accomplished.

Practical Actions

1. Set a Power Hour.
   Choose one 60-minute block each morning for your most important task, no distractions, no multitasking. Protect it like an appointment with your future self.

2. Use the Rule of Three.
   Each night, write your top three priorities for tomorrow. If an activity doesn't serve one of those three, delay or decline it.

3. Audit Your Attention.
   For one day, note how many times you check your phone, email, or messages. Awareness is the first step to reclaiming control of your focus.

In *The Foundation of Transformation*, you learned that energy flows where attention goes.

Focus is the daily practice of that truth. It's how design beats default, moment by moment, choice by choice. When you master focus, you master direction.

7. Faith

Faith is trusting the process before you see the results. It's believing that the invisible work you do today will bloom in its own time. Faith doesn't remove effort, it powers it.

When You Are In Faith, You:

- stay consistent even when progress feels slow.
- speak possibility instead of doubt.
- remind yourself that setbacks are detours, not dead ends.
- stay calm during uncertainty because you trust your foundation.
- take the next step even when the whole path isn't clear.

When You Are Not In Faith, You:

- give up after the first obstacle.
- question your path every time results aren't immediate.
- let fear or comparison dictate your mood.
- chase new ideas because patience feels uncomfortable.
- expect proof before commitment.

Practical Actions

1. Create a Proof List.
   Write down three moments from your past when something
   worked out after uncertainty. Read this list every time doubt
   appears, it reminds your brain that faith has evidence.

2. Use the "Next Step" Rule.
   When overwhelmed, stop asking "How will this all work?"
   and instead ask "What's my next step?" Faith grows with
   forward motion.

3. Plant and Water.
   Each morning, name one seed you're planting (an effort)
   and one way you'll water it (a follow-up action). Keep the
   rhythm; the results will catch up.

In *The Foundation of Transformation*, you learned that energy
requires both focus and flow. Faith is what sustains momentum
when outcomes are not yet visible. It transforms resistance into
trust and keeps your design alive when patience is tested. Faith
fuels endurance, the invisible engine of transformation.

8. Contribution

Contribution is giving your time, energy, or talent to something
beyond yourself.
It's how you turn personal growth into impact. When you
contribute, you expand because what you give multiplies.

When You Are In Contribution, You:

- share knowledge, skills, or encouragement without expecting credit.

- help someone solve a problem and feel energized, not drained.

- volunteer your time or resources to a cause that aligns with your values.

- look for ways to make your environment, home, work, community, better than you found it.

- speak kindly and uplift others, even when you're busy.

When You Are Not In Contribution, You:

- withhold help because "it's not my job."

- measure giving by what you'll get back.

- complain about problems instead of offering solutions.

- stay focused only on personal gain.

- forget that impact begins with small daily choices.

Practical Actions

1. Start Each Day with One Gift.
   Before checking your phone, send one encouraging message, share one idea, or thank one person. Begin your day by adding value to someone else's.

2. Choose a Weekly Contribution Zone.
    Pick one place to serve, a friend, family member, project, or local cause, and give one focused hour each week.

3. Notice Micro-Moments.
    Each evening, reflect: "Where did I make something better today?"
    Contribution doesn't always require time or money, sometimes it's a smile, a solution, or patience.

In *The Foundation of Transformation*, you learned to manage your energy and direct it with intention. Contribution is where that energy flows outward. It transforms self-awareness into service and turns growth into goodness. When you give from alignment, your energy renews itself. Generosity becomes expansion.

9. Authenticity

Authenticity is the courage to be real, to show up as who you are, not who you think you should be. It's living without disguise or performance. When you are authentic, your energy is clean, your message clear, and your presence magnetic.

When You Are In Authenticity, You:

- say what you mean, even when it's uncomfortable.
- make choices that reflect your true priorities, not what others expect.
- wear, speak, and live in a way that feels natural to you.
- admit mistakes instead of pretending to be perfect.
- attract relationships that feel easy because they're real.

When You Are Not In Authenticity, You:

- hide your opinions to avoid conflict or judgment.
- exaggerate success or mask struggle.
- say yes when you mean no.
- compare yourself to others and adjust to fit in.
- spend energy maintaining an image instead of building your truth.

Practical Actions

1. Run a Truth Check.
    When making a decision, pause and ask: "Is this true for me?"
    If your body feels heavy or tense, it's not aligned. If it feels light and steady, proceed.

2. Keep a Realness Journal.
    Write one short paragraph a day that begins with "What I really feel today is..."
    No edits, no filters, just honesty. It strengthens the muscle of self-truth.

3. One Honest Conversation a Week.
    Choose one person you trust and speak from the heart about something real, not rehearsed. Authenticity grows in spaces where honesty is safe.

In *The Foundation of Transformation*, you learned to clarify your values and understand your energy signature. Authenticity is living from that signature, letting your external life match your internal truth. When your expression and essence align, you no longer chase belonging; you embody it.

10. Legacy

Legacy isn't something you leave behind, it's something you build every day.
It's the sum of your choices, your character, and your contribution in motion.
Legacy is how your life continues to speak when you are not in the room.

When You Are In Legacy, You:

- live with intention, knowing that every action plants a seed.

- mentor, teach, or support others so your experience benefits more than just you.

- create work, relationships, and memories that uplift and outlast you.

- treat people and moments as emotional investments, not transactions.

- make decisions guided by values, not convenience.

When You Are Not In Legacy, You:

- live reactively, focused only on the next task or distraction.

- pursue recognition instead of meaning.

- keep wisdom to yourself instead of sharing it.

- break promises easily because you see them as temporary.

- think legacy begins later instead of realizing it starts now.

Practical Actions

1. Define Your Message.
    Write one sentence that completes this thought: "When people think of me, I want them to remember...". Keep it visible, it becomes your compass for decisions.

2. Give What You've Learned.
    Once a week, share one piece of knowledge or experience that could help someone else. Teaching magnifies your impact.

3. Design Small Moments of Meaning.
    Each day, ask: "What can I leave better today, a person, a space, or a moment?". Legacy is built in ordinary hours, not grand gestures.

Closing Reflection

In *The Foundation of Transformation*, you learned to design your life by intention and energy. Legacy is the proof of that design, it's what remains when habits become identity. It's the ripple effect of living by design, not by default. Legacy isn't future tense; it's how you live today, knowing it echoes tomorrow. And that's mastery.

Mastery is quiet. It's built in the small, repeated choices that shape your days and refine your energy. When you live these principles, you turn purpose into pattern and design into momentum.

"When we are no longer able to change a situation, we are challenged to change ourselves." Viktor Frankl

Live by Design, Not by Default.

PART 2

THE PRACTICE OF ALIGNMENT

"Nature does not hurry, yet everything is accomplished." Lao Tzu

In *Part 1 – The Practice of Mastery,* you learned how transformation gains structure and rhythm through ten guiding principles: Integrity, Responsibility, Accountability, Courage, Vision, Focus, Faith, Contribution, Authenticity, and Legacy. These principles formed the foundation of intentional living, the discipline that gives transformation its strength.

Part 2 – The Practice of Alignment builds on that foundation.
If mastery provides the framework, alignment refines how that framework moves.
Here, transformation becomes more deliberate and efficient, less about effort, more about ease.
It is the stage where discipline evolves into grace, where strong structure learns to flow.
In this section, you'll explore how to simplify, prioritize, and collaborate so that your actions stay aligned with your values and energy.
Alignment turns motion into harmony and strength into elegance, a state where your life feels both productive and peaceful.

1. Less Is More, *The Power of Eliminating and Delegating*

"Less is more" means choosing depth over quantity, clarity over clutter, and meaning over motion. It's about creating space in your schedule, mind, and energy so what truly matters can expand. You don't need to do more; you need to do what matters. The rest must be eliminated or delegated. Every "yes" costs energy; every unnecessary task steals clarity. Remember: "No" is a full sentence and you must use it often.

When You Live "Less Is More", You:

- stop trying to do everything and start doing the right things well.

- say no to what's merely good so you can say yes to what's great.

- simplify your environment, fewer open tabs, fewer possessions, fewer drains on energy.

- focus on completion, not collection, one finished project instead of five half-done ones.

- say no to what doesn't align with your goals, even when it feels uncomfortable.

- remove low-value tasks and hand off what others can do.

- know your strengths and you stay in your lane.

- clean your workspace, your schedule, and your digital life regularly.

- choose fewer, better, and finish what you start.

When You Forget "Less Is More", You:

- equate busyness with worth and mistake activity for progress.
- fill your home, your calendar, and your mind until you can't breathe.
- start everything, finish little, and wonder why nothing moves forward.
- take on too much and confuse helpfulness with importance.
- say yes out of guilt or habit and end up resentful.
- spend hours doing tasks someone else could do in 10 minutes.
- multitask and drain your energy trying to "keep up."
- confuse being busy with being valuable.

Practical Actions

1. The One-In, One-Out Rule.
    For every new item, commitment, or project you add,
    remove one. It keeps life light and energy clean.

2. The "Stop List."
    Each Friday, write down three things you will stop doing
    next week, tasks, habits, or obligations that add little value.

3. The Delegate Audit.
    Ask: "Does this require my unique ability?"

    - If yes, keep it.

    - If no, delegate, automate, or delete it.

In *The Foundation of Transformation*, you learned that energy
leaks through overcommitment. "Less Is More" closes those
leaks. It reminds you that design isn't about adding, it's about
aligning. When you remove the unnecessary, your focus, power,
and peace expand, and you learn that energy is finite and focus
is sacred. Eliminating and delegating protect the focus and the
energy. They keep you in design, not reaction. When you learn to
say no to what drains you, you say yes to your purpose.

2. Slow Is Fast

"Slow is fast" means doing things with full attention and right
timing instead of rushing through with half presence. It's not
about delay, it's about precision, rhythm, and mastery. When
you move slowly with awareness, you end up arriving sooner and
stronger.

When You Live "Slow Is Fast", You:

- build sustainable habits instead of chasing overnight results.

- take time to plan before acting and waste less energy correcting mistakes.

- listen fully before responding, so your relationships grow deeper.

- practice a skill with patience and notice that consistency outpaces intensity.

- rest intentionally, knowing recovery multiplies productivity.

When You Forget "Slow Is Fast", You:

- rush through tasks, then spend double the time fixing errors.

- multitask and call it efficiency but end the day scattered and exhausted.

- start ten things and finish none.

- push your body, your schedule, or your team past healthy limits and burn out instead of moving forward.

Practical Actions

1. Half-Speed Rule.
   Take one routine (eating, walking, writing, working out)
   and do it at half speed for one day. Notice how awareness
   increases precision.

2. Plan Before You Produce.
   Spend the first 10 minutes of each workday outlining your
   top priorities and the rest executing calmly.

3. Recovery Block.
   Schedule one 15 minute break for every 90 minutes of
   focused work. Use it to breathe, stretch, or walk. Rest is
   part of forward motion.

In *The Foundation of Transformation,* you learned that design
requires alignment and rhythm. "Slow Is Fast" is that rhythm, the
conscious pacing that keeps energy clean and direction clear. It
teaches that mastery isn't speed; it's steadiness. Progress built
slowly stays built.

3. Simple is Complex

Simplicity isn't the absence of depth, it's the mastery of it.
It's what you reach after exploring all the layers, all the noise,
and all the confusion. True simplicity is clarity earned through
understanding.

When You Live "Simple is Complex", You:

- stop overexplaining and start communicating clearly.

- create systems that are easy to follow because you've already done the hard thinking.

- know what matters most and focus on it.

- prefer quality over quantity, fewer goals, but deeper execution.

- simplify your habits, your business, and your decisions so your energy can flow.

When You Forget "Simple is Complex", You:

- overcomplicate everything, adding tools, rules, or steps that don't add value.

- hide behind complexity to feel safe or impressive.

- get stuck analyzing instead of doing.

- make decisions harder than they need to be.

- feel mentally scattered, always chasing a better method instead of trusting your clarity.

Practical Actions

1. Ask the Simplicity Question.
    Before every project or decision, ask: "How can I simplify this?" The answer reveals the truth and the shortcut.

2. Declutter One System.
    Simplify one area this week, your morning routine, your business workflow, or your email. Remove what adds no value and watch how much energy returns.

3. Teach to Test.
    Try explaining your idea or process to someone new. If you can't explain it simply, it's not yet clear. Keep refining until you can.

In *The Foundation of Transformation*, you learned that transformation begins with clarity and alignment. Simplicity is what follows. It's the sign you've integrated learning, not just collected it. Simplicity isn't reduction, it's resolution.

4. Team is a Multiplier

You can go fast alone, but you go far together. No great vision is built solo, every success has a structure of support behind it. A team is a multiplier: of time, of focus, of belief, of results, of life itself.

When You Live "Team is a Multiplier", You:

- ask for help before exhaustion arrives.
- surround yourself with people whose strengths complement yours.
- give credit freely and celebrate wins collectively.
- communicate clearly, delegate openly, and trust the process.
- invest time in relationships knowing that trust is built before it's needed.

When You Forget "Team is a Multiplier", You:

- try to do everything yourself and mistake control for competence.
- feel resentful because you're overextended and under-supported.
- don't communicate needs or boundaries, expecting others to read your mind.
- hold back ideas or feedback because you fear conflict.
- isolate under pressure instead of reaching out.

Practical Actions

1. Identify Your Core Circle.
   List three people who make you better, personally or professionally.
   Reach out this week with appreciation or collaboration in mind.

2. Play to Strengths.
   Ask yourself: "What do I do best?" and "What does someone else do better?" Delegate one task accordingly, that's leadership in action.

3. Weekly Connection Ritual.
   Schedule one intentional team moment, a check-in, gratitude message, or brainstorming call. Connection keeps momentum alive.

In *The Foundation of Transformation,* you learned that aligned energy multiplies impact.

The Power of Having a Team is multiplication in motion. It teaches that design is never meant to be a solo act, collaboration keeps vision alive, energy balanced, and purpose shared. You build faster when you build together.

5. Power over Force, The Energy of Synergy over the Chaos of Entropy

True power doesn't push; it aligns. It moves through harmony, not domination.
Force exhausts itself in resistance. Power regenerates through coherence. Force needs control, power flows through presence.

When you choose alignment over aggression, cooperation over control, you shift from entropy to synergy, from force to power. Power is quiet. Force is loud. Power flows from alignment; force fights against resistance. When you are in power, things move naturally. When you use force, you exhaust your energy trying to control them.

When You Live "Power over Force", You:

- speak calmly but your message carries weight.
- take aligned action and let results unfold instead of pushing outcomes.
- choose influence through integrity, not intimidation.
- listen more, react less, and move with grounded confidence.
- attract cooperation because your energy feels steady, not demanding.

When You Forget "Power over Force", You:

- push harder when things don't move instead of, stepping back to realign.
- argue to convince instead of connecting.
- exhaust yourself trying to control what isn't yours to control.
- let fear disguise itself as "drive."
- chase validation instead of embodying certainty.

Practical Actions

1. Pause Before You Push.
   When something feels heavy or stuck, stop. Ask, "Is this aligned or forced?"
   If it's forced, step back, breathe, and realign before acting.

2. Choose Influence, Not Control.
   Focus on your energy, not other people's reactions.
   Influence begins where control ends.

3. Create Power Habits.

   - Start your day with stillness, five minutes of quiet, gratitude, or breath.

   - End your day with release, write what's yours to carry and what's not.
     Power grows in presence, not pressure.

In *The Foundation of Transformation*, you learned that energy is your greatest currency.
Choosing power over force is how you spend it wisely. It's the state where clarity meets calm, and action meets flow. You stop pushing and start attracting.

Power is not what you do, it's how you *be*.

From Knowing to Living

Transformation is simple, not easy, but simple. You don't need more information; you need more implementation. The principles you just read are not theories; they are steppingstones of your human evolution.

The **first layer** gives you structure, the visible foundation of a life by design: **Integrity, Responsibility, Accountability, Courage, Vision, Focus, Faith, Contribution, Authenticity, Legacy.**

These are your anchors, they align your actions with your truth.

The **second layer** refines how you live this foundation.
Less Is More, Slow Is Fast, Simple is Complex, Team is a Multiplier, Power over Force. These are your rhythms, they keep your energy clean, your direction clear, and your motion graceful.

Your Practice for This Week

1. Choose one principle from each layer.
   Write them on paper where you'll see them daily.
   Example: Integrity and Less Is More.

2. Design one micro-action for each, something you can do today to live them.

   - Integrity → "I'll match my actions to my priorities."

   - Less Is More → "I'll remove one commitment that drains me."

3. Repeat for seven days. Small actions compound. One aligned week can change how you feel about your life.

Closing Reflection

Principles are the laws that keep your energy clean and your direction true.

They remind you that life doesn't need to be forced, it needs to be designed.
And design is harmony in motion.

When you live in alignment, you move through life with quiet confidence.
You stop chasing balance and start embodying it.
You no longer fight time; you flow with it.
This is the elegance of transformation, when your principles no longer feel like discipline, but like truth.

Transformation isn't built in theory; it's built in rhythm.
Be in integrity, move with courage, act with focus, and choose power over force.
That is how you build a life that feels whole and becomes your legacy.

When you reach this level of transformation, you stop chasing and start allowing.
You trust the current because you've become it.
You no longer strive to build momentum; you live as flow.

"When you do things from your soul, you feel a river moving in you, a joy." Rumi

Live by Design, Not by Default.

CHAPTER 4

THE TOOLS OF TRANSFORMATION

PART 1

TURNING AWARENESS INTO ACTION

"We are what we repeatedly do. Excellence, then, is not an act but a habit." Aristotle

Principles give us direction. Tools give us traction. The two belong together, one offers clarity, the other momentum. Without tools, principles remain abstract ideals; without principles, tools lose soul. Transformation is born at their meeting point, where awareness becomes practice and intention becomes motion.

Below is your toolkit. Each tool is a living instrument, a way to anchor awareness into your day, your routines, your energy. Some help you see more clearly; others help you act more consistently.
Together, they translate your philosophy into practice and your design into motion.

Transformation doesn't happen by accident. It happens by pattern.
And every pattern begins with one deliberate choice.

1. The Reflection Journal, Tool of Integration

The Reflection Journal is the space where wisdom settles. It converts moments into meaning, and patterns into awareness.

By writing, you witness your evolution. You track not just what you do, but who you are becoming. Reflection keeps you conscious, and consciousness keeps you on your path.

2. The Morning Ritual, Tool of Awakening

Every day begins with a choice, to react or to create. The Morning Ritual sets the tone for your energy, mindset, and intention. It is the time to connect before the world interferes. Whether through movement, gratitude, journaling, visualization, or stillness, this ritual is the ignition of your design. Begin your day as the architect of it, not its passenger.

3. The Energy Audit, Tool of Presence

Energy is your most precious currency. The Energy Audit helps you see how you spend it, which activities, thoughts, and people nourish you, and which deplete you. By bringing attention to your energetic balance, you learn to design your days with intention, not exhaustion. Presence grows naturally when your energy is managed consciously.

4. Life Inventory, Tool of Clarity

Before any change, you must see where you stand. Life Inventory is an honest snapshot of your current reality, your habits, relationships, finances, health, and emotional life. It turns vague unease into measurable awareness. It is not about judgment; it is about understanding. When you take inventory, you reclaim the power to design with precision rather than drifting by default.

5. The North Star Map, Tool of Direction

Once you know where you are, you must define where you're going. The North Star Map gives your goals orientation and your life a trajectory. It aligns vision with values and action with purpose. With it, daily decisions become part of something larger, each small choice guided by a single, steady light.

6. The Planning Practice, Tool of Design

If you fail to plan, you plan to fail. Planning is where clarity meets execution. It transforms scattered intention into a coherent path. Whether you design your week on Sunday or outline your top three priorities each morning, this practice is your anchor against distraction.

Planning is not rigidity; it is freedom created by foresight. It's how you build the bridge between vision and results, between dreaming and doing.

7. The Elimination and Delegation Matrix, Tool of Focus

Simplicity is power. The Elimination and Delegation Matrix clarifies what truly deserves your time. It's where you learn that "No" is a full sentence and that saying it often creates the space for your most important Yes. This tool teaches discernment: to release what is not yours to carry, and to delegate what dilutes your energy. Freedom begins when clutter ends.

8. The Action Calendar, Tool of Embodiment

Dreams require structure. The Action Calendar transforms intention into time. It bridges the abstract and the tangible, turning monthly visions into weekly priorities and daily rituals. When your goals have a visible rhythm, consistency becomes natural. This is how you embody your design: one day, one block of time, one deliberate action at a time.

9. The Willpower Compass, Tool of Consistency

Transformation doesn't happen in a day; it happens daily. The Willpower Compass helps you stay aligned through discipline and repetition. It is not about force; it is about direction. When clarity meets routine, willpower strengthens like a muscle. Every promise kept to yourself becomes another proof of strength, a small act of integrity reinforcing the next.

10. The Accountability Partnership, Tool of Multiplication

You rise higher with mirrors, not walls. The Accountability Partnership tool turns personal goals into shared responsibility. It transforms isolation into collaboration. When someone witnesses your commitment, celebrates your progress, and challenges your excuses, growth accelerates. A team is a multiplier. Shared energy becomes exponential power.

11. The Gratitude Ledger, Tool of Alignment

Gratitude magnifies abundance. The Gratitude Ledger helps you record what's already working, shifting focus from scarcity to sufficiency. Each entry strengthens emotional alignment, reminding you that fulfillment isn't found in the future but cultivated in the present. Gratitude does not deny challenges; it rebalances them with perspective.

12. The Evening Reset, Tool of Renewal

Every day deserves closure. The Evening Reset is a conscious ritual that clears mental and emotional residue before rest. It is a small ceremony of release and recalibration, reviewing what went well, what can improve, and what must be forgiven. Renewal begins in reflection. Tomorrow's energy is born from tonight's peace.

Everyday Design Practices: *Simple daily actions that turn awareness into momentum*

Transformation isn't built in theory; it's built in practice. The following four rituals are small, clear, and powerful. They don't require effort or perfection, only consistency and awareness.

Each of them strengthens a different area of your life:

Plan Your Day the Night Before builds awareness of your *intentions and priorities.*
Time Stamp Every Task builds awareness of how you use your *time and focus.*

Step on the Scale builds awareness of how you care for your *body and energy.*
Make Your Bed builds awareness of your *environment and discipline.*

Together, they create order, clarity, and confidence.
They remind you that small, intentional actions shape the rhythm of your entire life.

1. Plan Your Day the Night Before

Before you go to bed, take a few quiet minutes to plan your next day. Write it down, don't just think it.
There is something almost magnetic about words placed on paper. They gather energy and direction.
What you write down becomes a silent promise, a commitment between your mind and your future self.

Make your list, briefly go over it, and then put it aside where you can find it in the morning.
Go to sleep with a quiet and calm mind, knowing that everything is already captured, safe on paper, not circling in your thoughts.
Your rest will be deeper, your sleep healthier, and your morning clearer.

When you wake up, you'll already know what matters most. You'll move through your morning with intention instead of reaction.
A day planned in writing is a day already halfway won.

2. Time Stamp Every Task

Plan to put a time stamp on any task you do. It will completely change your relationship with time and teach you awareness and management.

Being aware of time, you achieve two things:
- You learn exactly how much each task truly takes, which helps you plan better next time.
– You experience the magic of time itself: when you are aware of time, time expands. When you are not, time shrinks.

How many times have you surprised yourself by how fast time passed? That's because you weren't present. Awareness brings you back into presence and mastery.

3. Step on the Scale Every Morning

Before brushing your teeth, plan to step on the scale and record the number on a small log kept nearby. This is not about judgment or chasing perfection, it is about awareness. Seeing the number teaches you how your body responds to different foods and habits.

It creates pull energy that helps you when temptation surrounds you. Over time, these daily data points will reveal your natural metabolism and guide your health and fitness goals far better than any diet plan will ever do.

4. Make Your Bed Every Morning

The moment you get out of bed, plan to make it. Not later, not after coffee, immediately. It's the first signal to your brain that order has begun. A made bed sets the tone for discipline, completion, and self-respect.

When your external world starts in alignment, your internal world follows. The act takes less than a minute, yet it tells your mind: *I am the designer of my day and my life.*

These simple rituals amplify your planning power instantly, awakening awareness that transforms ordinary routines into conscious design.

Closing Reflection

You've now entered the workshop of transformation, the place where intention becomes practice and ideas take shape. Each tool you've used, from the Reflection Journal to the Evening Reset is more than a habit; it's an act of self-creation.

We've already learned that transformation happens by pattern, not by accident. Every practice begins and ends with reflection and awareness, the quiet space where you pause, observe, and choose again. Awareness is the architect behind every design, the living current through which transformation becomes real.

These practices are the bridges between the invisible and the visible, the inner and the outer.
They remind you that transformation is not found in grand gestures, but in quiet consistency.

It's built in the moments when you choose awareness over autopilot, intention over impulse, design over default.

When you reflect, plan, act, and adjust, you teach life your rhythm, and life begins to respond in kind.

What once felt heavy starts to flow. What once required effort begins to move with ease.

That is the true power of these tools: they simplify complexity, turning change into pattern and pattern into peace.

You've learned how to do in alignment.
Now it's time to learn how to *be* in clarity.

"What is to give light must endure burning." Viktor Frankl

Live by Design, Not by Default.

PART 2

TURNING SELF-REFLECTION INTO CLARITY

The deepest transformation begins not when you act, but when you see.
Before building habits, systems, and structures that sustain your design, the first step is to turn inward into the quiet space where insight becomes illumination.

Self-reflection is the art of meeting yourself, honestly.
It's not self-criticism or analysis, but awareness in its purest form, the willingness to look within with compassion, curiosity, and truth.
Through reflection, emotion becomes information, and experience becomes wisdom.

The Tools that follow, *The Mirror* and *The Inner Dialogue,* are instruments of clarity. They reveal what drives you, what blocks you, and what still waits to be understood.
They teach you to pause, to listen, to translate reaction into awareness and awareness into growth.

Transformation without reflection is motion without meaning.
Reflection brings coherence, integrity, and light to all you've built so far.
It reminds you that the journey is not only about creation, but also, it is about understanding the creator.

1. The Mirror, Tool of Self-Reflection

"Knowing yourself is the beginning of all wisdom." Aristotle

Every moment of connection is a mirror. Every relationship, every reaction, every emotion shows us something about ourselves.

The way someone's tone affects us, the way we interpret silence, or even the way we give or withdraw, all of these are mirrors showing us something within. Every relationship reveals our hopes, wounds, insecurities, and capacities to love.

When we interact with others, we often think we're responding to them but most of the time we're reacting to what they reflect back to us. This is where the Mirror Tool comes in, the ability to see that what bothers us, what attracts us, and what moves us in others is, in some way, about us.

Projection vs. Reflection

When we project, our attention moves outward. We build stories about the other person, why they said what they said, what they felt, what they meant. These are assumptions, filtered through our own experiences and fears. Projection feels active, but it's passive; it keeps us powerless because we're trying to control something outside of us.

When we reflect, our attention turns inward. We ask: *"What is this situation showing me about myself?"* Reflection feels uncomfortable at first because it invites honesty but, that discomfort is the birthplace of growth. When we reflect, we move from blame to awareness. And reflection and awareness, as we are learning, are always the first two steps of transformation.

That is why the Mirror Tool is the heart of the Tool Series. Without the mirror, none of the other principles and tools can truly be lived.

- Integrity requires seeing ourselves clearly.
- Authenticity requires reflecting truthfully.
- Responsibility requires recognizing the reflection we create in others.

The mirror is the invisible thread connecting all three. It is how awareness turns into wisdom, and how wisdom turns into compassion.

Most of us spend our energy projecting instead of reflecting. Projection begins when we interpret the mirror as a window. We look outward and say:
"She did this because she's selfish."
"He said that because he's jealous."
"They're ignoring me because I'm not important."

Projection is fantasy, a story we build based on our own filters, fears, and assumptions. It makes us feel momentarily right but permanently powerless, because projection lives outside our control.

Reflection on the other hand is mastery. It brings back attention where power lives and that is inside us and not outside us. Reflection asks:
"What is this experience showing me about me?
"What feeling is being touched within me?"
"What do I need to learn, release, or realign?"

Projection wastes energy; reflection transforms it. Projection keeps us reactive; reflection makes us responsible.

When you reflect, you take ownership of your experience. You no longer spend hours decoding someone else's behavior; you decode your own emotions. You shift from analyzing others to understanding yourself.

And in that shift, from judgment to awareness, transformation begins. Because the first step of change is always seeing clearly. You cannot transform what you cannot see.

Reflection is clarity in motion. It's the bridge between emotion and evolution, between reaction and response

2. The Inner Dialogue, Tool of Turning Reaction Into Self-Reflection

This dialog was inspired by the ancient Greek art of rhetoric and self-inquiry. Have you ever experienced a negative inner dialogue about a person or situation that you couldn't stop? A noise in your head that grows louder the more you replay it, until it takes over your focus, your peace, your day. Of course you have. We all have. It's human.

Here is the tool that changes that noise, from something that consumes you into something that serves you.

It's called The Inner Dialogue. It transforms the mind's chatter into a conversation with awareness, a practice that turns reaction into reflection.

Imagine sitting quietly with yourself, heart open, mind curious. You become both the student and the teacher, both the one who asks and the one who answers. No noise, no audience, just you with yourself.

Then the dialogue begins:

Mind: Why do I feel so unsettled?
Heart: Because something touched a wound that wants to heal.
Mind: But I didn't do anything wrong. Why should I be the one hurting?
Heart: You are not being punished, you are being shown.
Mind: Shown what?
Heart: Where love is still missing within you.
Mind: But she said something unfair.
Heart: Yes, and it echoed a part of you that still believes you must prove your worth.
Mind: So it's not really about her?
Heart: It never is. The mirror only shows what's already inside.
Mind: Then what should I do with what I see?
Heart: Stay. Breathe. Feel it. The mirror does not ask for judgment, it asks for honesty.
Mind: And if I don't like the reflection?
Heart: Then polish it with awareness, forgiveness, and gentleness. That is how clarity turns into peace.

This is the practice of reflection, the ancient dialogue between awareness and emotion, logic and compassion, shadow and light. When you practice it regularly, emotional storms turn into lessons. You learn to pause before reacting, to ask before assuming, to see before deciding. The mirror stops being a threat and becomes a teacher.

You can use this rhetorical dialogue anytime: after a conversation that lingers, when a memory stirs, when an emotion repeats. Simply open your journal or your heart and ask: *What am I seeing? What is this showing me about me?* Let the dialogue unfold naturally. The mirror will answer in truth, not judgment.

Practical Actions

1. Notice the Projection.
   Each time you catch yourself saying, *"They made me feel...,"* pause. Replace it with, *"I felt... because..."* This simple shift turns projection into reflection and restores your power.

2. Keep a Mirror Journal.
   Write one short dialogue per week. Describe a situation that triggered emotion, then let both voices speak, your Mind and your Heart. Read it again after a few days. You'll see wisdom forming between the lines.

3. Practice the Pause.
   When emotion rises, pause before reacting. Breathe. Ask: *"What is this really showing me about me?"* That single pause is the space where transformation begins.

4. Use the Mirror with Compassion.
   The mirror is not a weapon. Do not use it to criticize yourself or others. Use it to understand, to release, to grow. Self-awareness without kindness becomes self-judgment; awareness with love becomes liberation.

The Mirror is Your Doorway for Growth

In *The Foundation of Transformation,* you learned that clarity precedes mastery, and energy follows awareness. The Mirror Tool is where those truths meet. It is clarity in action, awareness embodied.

Integrity lives through reflection, and Authenticity is born from it. Without reflection, integrity becomes theory; with reflection, it becomes truth. Without reflection, authenticity becomes performance; with reflection, it becomes presence.

The mirror is the mechanism of alignment. It turns every interaction into a doorway for growth, and every emotion into a compass for healing.

Every soul you meet is a mirror. Every moment of conflict, love, or silence is an invitation to see yourself more clearly. The mirror does not lie, it reveals.

When you look with courage, you find truth. When you look with love, you find freedom.

Transformation begins the moment you stop trying to change the mirror and start polishing it. What you polish inside will shine everywhere outside.

We don't really see people as they are; we see them as we are. And they, in turn, reflect us back, through love, through conflict, through silence.

This is how reflection reveals truth and freedom:
Reflection + Awareness + Clarity + Alignment + Action + Rhythm = TRANSFORMATION

This is The Transformation Formula.

It's a living practice.

It's a formula that works if you do.

Closing Reflection

You've completed the journey, not to an ending, but to a beginning.
You've traveled from reflection and awareness to embodiment, from clarity to creation, from knowing to becoming.

You learned to see with honesty, to choose with intention, to act with alignment, and to live with energy.
You've built principles that hold your integrity and tools that carry your truth.

And somewhere between discipline and grace, reflection and action, you became your own designer.

Transformation is not a single act; it's a rhythm: **Reflection, Awareness, Clarity, Alignment, Action, Rhythm.**
It's a pulse that repeats, each time more natural, more effortless, truer.

When you live by design, you stop waiting for change and start creating it.
You stop chasing balance and start embodying harmony.
You realize that the Phoenix doesn't rise once, it rises again and again, each time lighter, wiser, and freer.

You are that Phoenix.
You are the artist and the art.
You are both the design and the designer.

Protect your energy. Honor your principles. Use your tools.
And remember: your life expands in direct proportion to your awareness of it.

This is how transformation becomes a way of being,
day by day, choice by choice,
living life by design, not by default.

"Everything that irritates us about others can lead us to an understanding of ourselves." Carl Jung

Live by Design, Not by Default.

CHAPTER 5:

The Legacy

The Transformation Formula

Reflection + Awareness + Clarity + Alignment + Action + Rhythm

= *Transformation*

The Language of Symbols

Since the dawn of humanity, long before we had alphabets or philosophies, we had symbols.
Carved into stone, painted on cave walls, danced around sacred fires, symbols carried what words could not.
They spoke to the heart, not the mind.
They guided us through mystery, meaning, and becoming.

To this day, symbols move us because they speak the language of the soul.
They awaken memory older than thought.
They stir emotion, ignite intuition, and remind us of our eternal nature.
When emotion and thought meet, transformation begins, this is the alchemy of becoming.

My work is rooted in that language.
I use symbols not as decoration, but as *doorways*.
Each one, the Phoenix, the Butterfly, the Alchemist, the North Star and the Compass, represents a path of inner evolution.
They help us remember that transformation is not learned; it is lived.
It is felt in the fire, the unfolding, and the creation of something new.

Symbols are the quiet language of the soul.
They speak through energy, imagery, and intuition, reaching places that words cannot.
Each one carries a meaning, a vibration, and a reminder of who you are becoming.

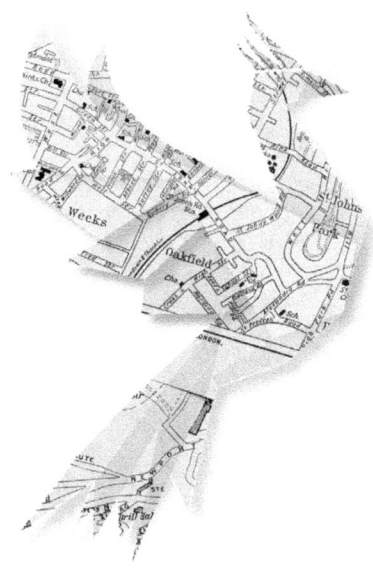

The Phoenix

The Phoenix represents rebirth and resilience.
It is the fire of transformation, the courage to release what no longer serves and rise renewed from your own ashes.
It reminds you that nothing is ever truly lost. Everything can be reborn through awareness and will.

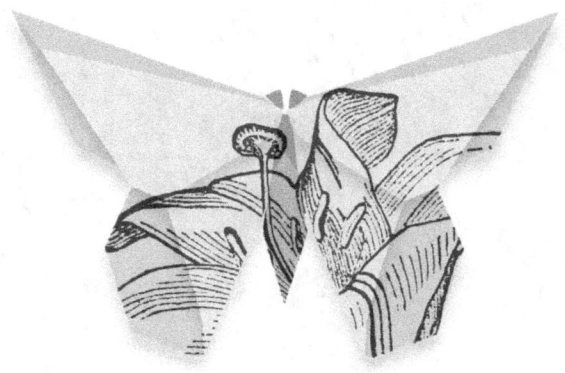

The Butterfly
The Butterfly embodies transformation and grace.
It is the symbol of surrender and gentle evolution, of trusting the cocoon and emerging into freedom.
It teaches that growth does not need to be forced. It can unfold softly, beautifully, and in divine timing.

The Alchemist
The Alchemist stands for conscious creation.
It is the power to turn intention into form, energy into matter, and challenges into wisdom.
It reminds you that you are the artist of your life, shaping reality through clarity, focus, and will.

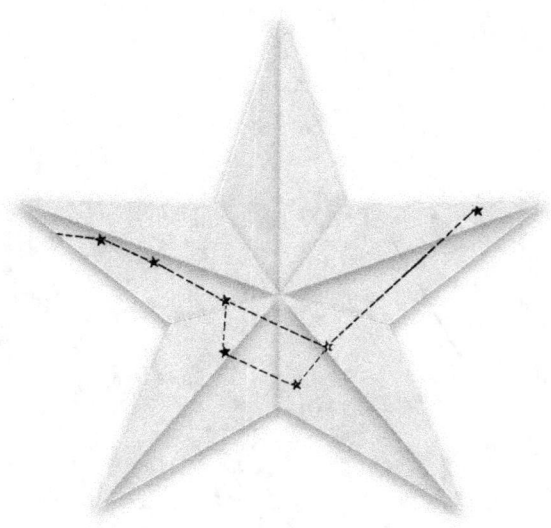

The North Star
The North Star symbolizes purpose and direction.
It is the steady light that guides you home when the path feels
uncertain.
It teaches that you already know the way. You only need to look
up, remember your truth, and trust your own light.

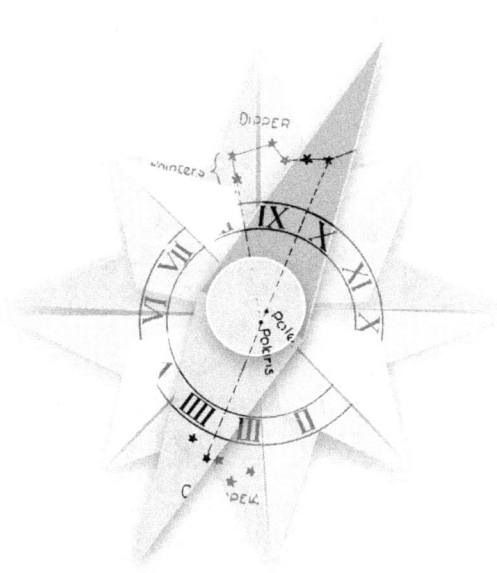

The Compass

The Compass represents integrity and alignment.
It is your inner guidance system, the magnetic pull of your values
and needs that always points you back to authenticity.
It reminds you to choose what feels right, not just what looks
right, and to live in alignment with your deepest truth.

Together, these five symbols form the sacred alphabet of transformation, the Phoenix rising, the Butterfly unfolding, the Alchemist creating, the North Star guiding, and the Compass aligning.

Through my writing, my coaching, and my retreats, I invite people to walk these paths, to see their lives as art, their struggles as raw material, and their growth as sacred design.
Symbols are the bridge between who we have been and who we are becoming.

Yet, even beyond symbols lies something more elemental. Love, People, and Time. They are not metaphors but living energies, the forces that give every story its pulse. They shape how we create, connect, and remember.
Symbols help us see; these forces help us live.
They turn awareness into experience and meaning into legacy.

The Three Forces of Life: Love, People, and Time

"It is not that we have a short life, but that we waste much of it." Seneca

Above all principles and tools, beyond every habit or formula, **Love, People, and Time** give meaning to everything we do.

Everything begins with *love*, the silent current behind every action, the energy that fuels every transformation. It moves through people, across time, through every heartbeat and creation.
Everything matters because of *people*, those we love, those we serve, those who shape our journey.
And everything is measured through *time,* our most precious, non-renewable resource, given to us only once.

The universe is around **13.8 billion years old.**
Our planet, approximately **4.8 billion.**
And our human life, even at **90 years**, is less than the blink of an eye in cosmic time.
Yet within that blink lies the entirety of our experience, the laughter, the love, the creation, the transformation.

Now let's look at it as a formula.

If you live to be **90 years old**, that's **32,850 days**.
You spend about **one-third** of that sleeping, **30 years.**
Another third working, studying, or caring for others, that's **30 years.**

That leaves roughly **30 years** of *awake, personal, self-directed life.*

In reality, much of that time is scattered, commuting, recovering, doing what must be done.
So, on average, what we truly *live consciously for ourselves* may be closer to **25 years.**
Just **one-quarter** of our lifespan, a single slice of existence that holds the potential to define our legacy.

That's the **Formula of Life**:
90 years = 30 sleeping + 30 working/caring + 30 living ≈ **25 years truly yours.**

When you see it this way, everything shifts.
You begin to guard your time like treasure, to fill it with meaning, creation, and love.
You start to realize that the real success is not what you build, but *how much love and presence you bring* to the brief time you have.

Because when love guides us, time expands.
When people matter, life deepens.
And when we honor both, we live by design, awake, grateful, and free.

Quote: *"He aha te mea nui o te ao? He tāngata, he tāngata, he tāngata."* Māori proverb

"What is the most important thing in the world? It is people, it is people, it is people."

Love by Design, Not by Default.

EPILOGUE: THE BEGINNING WITHIN

Every journey begins with a vibration, a single thought, a note of awareness that awakens something within.
This book began in a concert hall by the sea, surrounded by Strauss's *Metamorphosen.*
Your journey of transformation begins here, in the place you stand and the moment you decide.
Transformation is not the end of a path; it is the beginning of living awake.

You have now seen the architecture of design, the clarity, the direction, the energy, and the rhythm of mastery. From here, your work is simple: to live it, to act on it.

Every moment is a page in the unwritten part of your story. Every breath is a chance to return to design.
The Phoenix is within you.
The Butterfly, unfolding.
The Alchemist, creating.
The Compass, aligning.
And your North Star still shines, quietly waiting for your next step.

To transform is to act.
Awareness without action is only potential.
Feeling without expression is only echo.

As the wise master once said, *"Do. Or do not. There is no try."*
Yoda

Trying is hesitation disguised as movement. Doing is presence in motion, the alignment of intention and will. Every transformation requires a step, a gesture, a choice.

And when you forget, as we all do, come back here. Read again. Reflect again. Begin again.

Because every ending is only a beginning in disguise, and your next chapter is already waiting for you to turn the page.

The symphony has ended, but its vibration lives in you now.
Listen for it.
Live by it.
And let it remind you that you are the music now.
Do. Create. Become.

Live by Design, Not by Default.

MARIA FRANCU

Born beneath gray skies and watchful eyes in communist Romania, Maria dreamed of a freer life and made it real. Her path has been one of fire and flight, of falling and rising, each time closer to truth.

A life coach, entrepreneur, writer, and world traveler, Maria blends psychology, spirituality, and art to help people live intentionally and rise from their own ashes. Born with a heart defect and raised in a system that tried to limit her, she learned early what pain, fear, and courage truly mean. Her own transformation became the foundation of her life's work, guiding others to rebuild, realign, and rise.

After her chapter at Columbia University and Chase Manhattan Bank, Maria shifted from corporate success to conscious entrepreneurship, creating housing and hope for those facing life's hardest challenges, homelessness, disability, single parenthood, and veteran reintegration. Over time, she evolved from rebuilding homes to rebuilding lives, helping others design transformation through clarity, energy, and purpose.

Through her brand *Live by Design, Not by Default*, Maria invites others to awaken their inner Phoenix, unfold like the Butterfly, create like the Alchemist, align with their Compass, and follow their North Star. Her work, through writing, one on one coaching, and group coaching retreats is an invitation to rise, live with intention, and become the architect of one's own life.

Her debut book, *The Transformation Formula: How to Create Your Own Luck and Win the Lottery of Life*, is both a guide and a gift, a practical, yet soulful system for designing a life you love.

She divides her time between the ocean's edge in Delaware and the wider world, coaching, organizing coaching retreats, writing, dancing, guiding others toward lives of energy, integrity, and joy.

Visit ignitemotivation.com or follow Maria Francu on social media for reflections, retreats, and inspiration.

ACKNOWLEDGMENTS

To my parents,
who gave me life, resilience, and faith,
the soil from which every dream could rise.
Your sacrifices are the quiet architecture beneath my wings.

To my daughters, Theodora and Tiffany,
you are my why, my wonder, and my wings.

To my friends, mentors, and the unseen hands of grace,
you reminded me that transformation is never solitary;
it is the universe conspiring through people, moments, and
miracles.

To every soul who walked beside me,
in light or in shadow,
in love or in lesson,
thank you.

And to Life itself,
for breaking me open only to reveal more light.